Standardized Assessment Tutor

HOLT, RINEHART AND WINSTON

A Harcourt Classroom Education Company

Austin · New York · Orlando · Atlanta · San Francisco · Boston · Dallas · Toronto · London

Contributing Writer

Sandra Brashier

Copyright © by Holt, Rinehart and Winston

All rights reserved. No part of this publication may be reproduced or transmitted in any form or by any means, electronic or mechanical, including photocopy, recording, or any information storage and retrieval system, without permission in writing from the publisher.

Teachers using ¡VEN CONMIGO! may photocopy complete pages in sufficient quantities for classroom use only and not for resale.

Cover Photo Credits:
© Jose L Pelaez/Corbis Stock Market.

¡VEN CONMIGO! is a trademark licensed to Holt, Rinehart and Winston, registered in the United States of America and/or other jurisdictions.

Printed in the United States of America

ISBN 0-03-065998-1

1 2 3 4 5 6 7   066   05 04 03 02 01

Table of Contents

To the Teacher iv
Test-Taking Strategies
   General Test-Taking Strategies.. vi
   Reading.. vii
   Writing viii
   Math ix
   Overcoming Test Anxiety x

Standardized Assessment Practice

Capítulo 1
Reading Test 1
Writing Test 4

Capítulo 2
Reading Test 5
Writing Test 8

Capítulo 3
Reading Test 9
Writing Test 12

Capítulo 4
Reading Test 13
Writing Test 16

Capítulo 5
Reading Test 17
Writing Test 20

Capítulo 6
Reading Test 21
Writing Test 24

Math Test 1 25

Capítulo 7
Reading Test 27
Writing Test 30

Capítulo 8
Reading Test 31
Writing Test 34

Capítulo 9
Reading Test 35
Writing Test 38

Capítulo 10
Reading Test 39
Writing Test 42

Capítulo 11
Reading Test 43
Writing Test 46

Capítulo 12
Reading Test 47
Writing Test 50

Math Test 2 51

Score Sheets
   (Reading, Writing, Math) 55

Answer Key 57

To the Teacher

Teachers in all disciplines are being called upon to help prepare students to take standardized reading, writing, and math tests. As a language teacher, you are already targeting many of the same skills that your students will need in order to perform well on standardized tests. Using the *¡Ven conmigo! Standardized Assessment Tutor*, your students can practice Spanish while preparing to take standardized tests in English.

The practice tests in this book are presented in a format similar to many state-approved standardized tests. If your students are familiar with the test formats, they may experience lower levels of anxiety and therefore perform better when faced with an actual test. Because the reading selections, writing topics, and mathematical concepts targeted in this book mirror the linguistic and cultural content presented in the chapters of *¡Ven conmigo!*, students will remain focused on Spanish while preparing for standardized tests in other disciplines.

Following the tests is a two-page score sheet that can be photocopied and used with each reading, writing, and math test. There is an answer key for each chapter.

The *¡Ven conmigo! Standardized Assessment Tutor* also includes strategies for taking reading, writing, and math tests. You may want to remind students to use specific strategies before you give each practice test.

Reading Tests

Each chapter contains three practice reading tests. Your students will read a variety of selections, including narratives, dialogues, letters, and realia. Each reading passage is followed by a series of multiple-choice questions that ask students to perform the kinds of tasks they will perform when taking standardized reading tests, such as identifying facts and details, inferring information, making predictions, and finding main ideas. At the same time, your students will be given the opportunity to apply the reading strategies, such as skimming and scanning, they have been learning in your language class. The following is an excerpt from one of the practice reading tests.

A. Read Alicia's letter to her friend María Inés and answer the questions that follow. (20 points)

Querida María Inés,

Hola, ¿cómo estás? ¿Cómo son tus clases? Yo tengo algunas clases que me gustan mucho. Por la mañana tengo matemáticas, francés y geografía. Luego por la tarde tengo ciencias sociales, arte y educación física. El arte y el francés son mis clases favoritas. ¿Cuál es tu clase favorita?

1 Which of these classes does Alicia have in the morning?
   A French
   B art
   C gym
   D social studies   (correct answer: French)

Writing Tests

The practice writing tests target several of the written composition objectives articulated for standardized writing tests in English. In addition to writing dialogues and letters, your students will have the opportunity to develop their narrative, expository, and persuasive writing skills. Here is an example taken from one of the practice writing tests.

> **Persuasive writing** It is the first day of school and you arrive home with a list of materials that you need to buy at the book store. The list must include at least five things that you will buy. Tell your mom that you need money to buy these things. Tell her where you will buy these items. Also inform her that you want to be more organized this school year. You should write at least 5 sentences. (15 points)

Math Tests

Each level of the *¡Ven conmigo! Standardized Assessment Tutor* includes two practice math tests that target math concepts related to the cultural topics your students will learn in class, such as using the metric system to measure height, weight, and distances. Based on illustrations and graphs, students will solve equations to perform tasks like currency and temperature conversions. As your students practice math, they will also further develop their ability to function within a Spanish-speaking society. The following is an example from one of the practice math tests.

> The temperatures in the chart below are given in degrees Celsius. Use the formula $T_F = \frac{9}{5} t_c + 32.0$ to convert temperatures from Celsius to Fahrenheit. (T_F = temperature in Fahrenheit; t_c = temperature in Celsius) Make sure to round your answers to the nearest whole number.

PRONÓSTICO: ESPAÑA   el 18 de marzo

Ciudad	hoy mínimo/máximo °C	mañana mínimo/máximo °C
La Coruña	15/19	15/17
Barcelona	14/20	13/25
Córdoba	9/24	9/25
Jaén	6/22	7/24
Madrid	12/17	11/19
Málaga	10/23	11/26
Sevilla	11/24	10/25
Valencia	17/21	17/23

1 What is the high temperature tomorrow in Seville?

  A 43° F

  B 52° F

  C 75° F

  D 77° F   (correct answer: D)

Because the content of the practice tests is closely tied to what your students are already learning in class, they will remain focused on your course objectives as they prepare to be tested in other disciplines.

To the Student: Test-Taking Strategies

If you are among the many students who would like to do well on standardized tests but who frequently go blank when taking them, you may want to arm yourself with some test-taking strategies. The suggestions below can help you feel more confident and perform better on standardized reading, writing, and math tests.

General Test-Taking Strategies

Read directions carefully.

Make sure you understand what you're supposed to do in each section of a test. If you're not sure, ask for clarification. Don't try to guess what the directions mean and don't make assumptions.

Don't spend too much time on one question.

If you don't know the answer to a question, don't waste valuable time on it. Move on to the next question. When answering a series of questions about a single topic, a later question may provide a clue. Mark any questions you skip so you don't forget to come back to them.

Use the process of elimination.

Read all of the choices before marking your answer. Eliminate those that are obviously incorrect, then choose the best answer from the remaining choices.

Use all of the time available.

If you finish a test and you still have some time left, check your work. Re-check your answers and proofread. Use any extra time to eliminate careless mistakes.

Be prepared.

Nothing builds your test-taking confidence like knowing that you're prepared. As you study, mentally "quiz yourself" by asking yourself questions. If you don't readily know the answers, study some more!

Be informed.

Find out about the test beforehand. Ask your teacher what you'll need to know and what kind of questions you'll be asked. Taking practice tests can help you prepare for the actual test. Being familiar with the format of a test can help you feel more at ease.

Strategies for Reading Tests

The main goal of the reading sections of standardized tests is to determine your understanding of the reading passage. Questions may focus on the main idea, or they may check your understanding of the details of the passage. A correct answer may be stated clearly in the text, or you may have to make inferences and draw conclusions based on information provided.

Look at the big picture.

Examine the most obvious features of the text. Decide what type of reading selection it is. Is it an article, a letter, or perhaps an advertisement? What do pictures or illustrations tell you? Look for information in titles and headings.

Read the entire passage before answering questions.

Skim the selection to get a general overview of the topic and the tone of the passage. If you do not understand at first, keep reading. At this point, focus on understanding the main idea of the passage. Consider details later.

Read the questions.

Read all of the questions so you'll know what information to look for when you reread the passage. Don't read the answer choices and don't mark any answers yet.

Re-read the passage.

Once you have a general idea of what the passage is about and you know what the questions are, read the passage a second time. As you reread, underline any information that relates to the questions.

Answer the questions in your own words.

Try to answer each question in your mind before considering the answer choices, then look for a similar answer among the choices provided. Be sure to read *all* of the answer choices and mark the best one.

When in doubt, read again.

If the answer you expected is not among your choices, return to the passage. Look especially at any sections you underlined. Check for any words you may have misunderstood. Use context to help you figure out what they mean.

Make your best guess.

If you've completed the steps above and you're still not sure, mark the answer that seems most likely to be correct. Ask your teacher if you should answer every question or if you are penalized for guessing.

Strategies for Writing Tests

The main goal of a writing test is to determine your ability to express yourself clearly. Clear writing is well-organized and free of grammatical and spelling errors.

Determine the purpose of your writing.

You may be asked to write for a variety of purposes. For example, writing assignments may require you to describe something, to tell a story, or to support an opinion. Decide what the purpose of each assignment is and remain focused on that purpose as you write.

Create a brief outline.

Before you begin writing, gather your thoughts. Briefly outline the main points you want to include and put your ideas in order. List any vocabulary words you'll want to use.

Write a topic statement.

Write a single sentence that clearly states the main idea of your writing. You may or may not include this sentence in your finished assignment. Its purpose is to keep you focused on the writing task.

Think of a title.

Like a topic statement, a title can keep you focused on your writing purpose, even if you revise it later or eliminate it completely from your finished product.

Write thoughtfully and completely.

Follow directions carefully and make sure your writing assignment is complete. If you have time, double-check by rereading directions after you've finished writing. Remember, most types of writing should have an introduction, a body, and a conclusion. Letters should contain a greeting and some kind of closing at the end.

Use your imagination.

When creating a story or other type of writing for a test, you need not tell the truth or give details about your own life. Try writing from the point of view of someone else. Using your imagination is fun and it can save you valuable time during a test. For example, if you can't remember how to say *dog*, you can say *cat* instead.

Read it. When you've finished writing, read what you've written. Make sure it makes sense and flows well. Add any details you may have left out.

Proofread it. Reread your work to check for grammar and spelling errors. If you have time, you may want to read it several times, looking for a different type of error each time.

Strategies for Math Tests

The purpose of a math test is to determine your ability to perform mathematical functions, such as addition, subtraction, multiplication, and division, to solve equations.

List the given and unknown values.

You may be asked to solve word-problems or derive information from graphs or charts. In any case, some of the information you'll need to solve the problem will be provided. First, list the information that is provided, (the given values), then what information is missing (the unknown values).

Given values: value of 1 Canadian dollar = $1.50 US currency
                       price of a book in Canadian dollars = $16.50

Unknown value: price of the book in US dollars = ?

Write out the equation.

Math problems must be converted into equations in order to be solved. To calculate the price of the book in US currency, you'd need to solve the following equation.

price of book ÷ value of 1 Canadian dollar = price of book in US currency

Insert the known values into the equation.

Once you know what the equation is, you can plug in the information you need to solve it. For the currency conversion described above, the equation is as follows:

$16.50 ÷ $1.50 = _____

Solve the equation.

To solve the equation, perform the necessary multiplication, division, addition, or subtraction as needed. Remember to show your work if required.

$16.50 ÷ $1.50 = $11.00

Recheck your answer.

Whenever possible, recheck your work by working the problem in a different way. For example, to check your division, multiply one of the items divided ($16.50 or $1.50) by your answer ($11.00). The result should be the other item.

original problem: 16.50 ÷ 1.50 = 11.00   recheck: 11.00 x 1.50 = 16.50

Evaluate your solution.

Make sure your solution answers the question asked. Ask yourself whether or not your answer makes sense.

Overcoming Test Anxiety

Test-taking makes many people a little anxious, but you can use strategies to overcome your worries and perform better on tests.

Be well-prepared physically.

You should arrive at a test well-rested and well-fed. Get a good night's sleep and be sure to set your alarm. Lack of sleep and poor nutrition can hurt your ability to concentrate.

Talk to your teacher about your feelings.

If you're feeling anxious about a test, tell your teacher how you're feeling. Ask what you can do to feel better prepared. Your teacher knows your abilities well and is likely to be able to give some personalized suggestions to help you.

Don't be distracted by other students.

Focus on your own performance on the test. Sit in a place where you won't be distracted by your classmates. Don't worry if others finish before you. A smart test-taker uses any extra time to recheck answers.

Avoid negative discussions with other students.

While studying with others is a good idea, do not indulge in discussions about how worried you are or how unfair your situation seems. Such talk is not helpful and it will only increase your anxiety.

Have a positive attitude.

As you begin to take a test, think positively. Remind yourself that you have studied well and that you are prepared. Negative thoughts can interfere with your performance, so push them right out of your head!

Relax.

As you wait for the test to begin, remind yourself of all the things you've done to prepare. Take a deep breath, relax, and do your best.

Standardized Assessment Practice

CAPÍTULO 1

¡Mucho gusto!

I. Reading

(Maximum score: 60 points)

A. Read the letter that your pen pal sent you. Then, choose the correct answer for the questions that follow. (20 points)

> Hola,
>
> ¿Qué tal? Me llamo Antonio García Conde. Soy de Barcelona, España. Tengo quince años. Me gusta mucho el baloncesto, pero me gusta más la natación. También me gusta la clase de inglés, pero no me gusta la tarea.
>
> ¿Y tú? ¿Cuántos años tienes? ¿Qué te gusta?
>
> Bueno, chao.
>
> Antonio

1 How old is the person writing the letter?
  A five
  B fifty
  C fifteen
  D He doesn't say.

2 What is Antonio's favorite sport?
  F swimming
  G He doesn't have a favorite sport.
  H He likes all sports.
  J basketball

3 How does Antonio feel about his English class?
  A He likes to do the homework.
  B He doesn't like the class.
  C He likes the class but not the homework.
  D The homework it too difficult.

4 Which of the following in *not* a true statement?
  F The person writing the letter is Antonio.
  G The person writing the letter is from Spain.
  H The person writing the letter is learning English.
  J The pen pals have been writing for a long time.

5 What information does Antonio want from his pen pal?
  A what country he is from
  B why he doesn't like homework
  C in which subjects he does well
  D his age and what he likes

Spanish 1 ¡Ven conmigo!, Chapter 1   Standardized Assessment Tutor **1**

B. Marisela is a new student at the Colegio Obregón. Read the following interview with her that appeared in the school newspaper. Based on what you read, decide which of the following is the correct answer. (20 points)

REPORTERO   ¿Cómo estás, Marisela?
MARISELA   Estoy bien, gracias.
REPORTERO   ¿De dónde eres y cuántos años tienes?
MARISELA   Bueno, soy de México, D.F., y tengo catorce años.
REPORTERO   ¿Y qué te gusta?
MARISELA   Bueno, me gusta mucho la música.
REPORTERO   ¿La música rock?
MARISELA   Pues, sí, me gusta la música rock, pero me gusta más la música clásica. También me gusta el jazz.
REPORTERO   ¿Y te gusta el fútbol?
MARISELA   No, no me gusta el fútbol, pero el voleibol me gusta mucho.
REPORTERO   Bueno, Marisela, gracias, y bienvenida *(welcome)*.
MARISELA   Gracias. Chao.

6 How old is Marisela?
  A four years old
  B fourteen years old
  C forty years old
  D She doesn't tell the reporter.

7 What is Marisela's favorite type of music?
  F jazz
  G classical
  H rock
  J She doesn't have a favorite type of music.

8 Which of the following is *not* a true statement?
  A Marisela is from Mexico City.
  B Marisela likes music.
  C Marisela likes soccer better than volleyball.
  D Marisela doesn't like all sports.

9 Which sport does Marisela like best?
  F all sports
  G football
  H soccer
  J volleyball

10 Which question does the reporter *not* ask Marisela?
  A Where are you from?
  B How do you like living in Mexico?
  C How old are you?
  D What do you like?

Nombre _____ Clase _____ Fecha _____

C. Read the following letter, and then answer the following questions. (20 points)

> *Querido Felipe,*
>
> *Me llamo Rafael y soy de Cuernavaca, México. Me gusta mucho el fútbol, y también el fútbol norteamericano. No me gusta el tenis. Me gusta mucho la música rock, pero no me gusta mucho ni el pop ni la música clásica. La ensalada no me gusta, pero me gusta mucho la comida italiana. ¿Qué te gusta a ti?*
>
> *Hasta luego,*
> *Rafael*

CAPÍTULO 1

11 Which sport does Rafael *not* like?
  A all sports
  B tennis
  C soccer
  D football

12 Which type of music does Rafael like best?
  F all types
  G pop music
  H classical music
  J rock

13 Which of the following is *not* a true statement about Rafael?
  A He doesn't like classical music very much.
  B He likes to speak Italian.
  C He is from Cuernavaca, Mexico.
  D Rafael and Felipe are not old friends.

14 What food does Felipe like?
  A salad
  B Italian food
  C all types of food
  D He doesn't say in this letter.

15 What does Rafael want to know about Felipe?
  A what he likes
  B why he likes football
  C how old he is
  D where he is from

Spanish 1 ¡Ven conmigo!, Chapter 1   Standardized Assessment Tutor **3**

Nombre _____ Clase _____ Fecha _____

II. Writing   (Maximum score: 40 points)

Answer the following questions in the space provided.

16 Descriptive writing You are to write a report for your Spanish class about yourself. Be sure to include your name, your age, and where you are from. Include your favorite sport and the sport that you don't like. Be sure to include at least one of your favorite foods or types of food and one that you don't like. (15 points)

_____
_____
_____
_____
_____
_____
_____

17 Narrative writing Write a letter to a pen pal in another country. Be sure to include a greeting and a farewell. Introduce yourself, including your name, your age, where you are from, what you like to do, and what you don't like to do. Ask about your pen pal's age and likes and what he or she is like. (15 points)

_____,
_____
_____
_____
_____
_____
_____
                                            _____

18 Comparative writing. Everyone has likes and dislikes. Write a brief report about yourself, including your name, your age, and where you are from. Write about two things that you like and two things that you don't like. (10 points)

_____
_____
_____
_____
_____
_____
_____

CAPÍTULO 1

¡Organízate!

I. Reading
(Maximum score: 60 points)

A. Read this letter from Isabel to her friend Juana. Then, answer the following questions based on the reading. (20 points)

> Querida Juana,
> ¡Hola! ¿Qué tal? Yo estoy bien, pero necesito hacer muchas cosas. Mañana es el primer día de clases en el colegio, y mi cuarto es un desastre. Necesito organizar mi ropa en el armario y encontrar mis zapatillas de tenis. También necesito organizar los papeles en mi escritorio. Quiero ir a la librería para comprar unos bolígrafos, unos lápices y una regla. Como tengo dinero, quiero comprar una mochila y una revista también.
> Y tú, ¿necesitas hacer muchas cosas también?
> Hasta luego,
> Isabel

1. What does Isabel need to do?
   A finish her homework for tomorrow
   B study for a test
   C get ready for a tennis tournament
   D get organized for the first day of classes

2. What does Isabel *not* need to buy?
   F pens
   G a ruler
   H tennis shoes
   J a backpack

3. Where does Isabel go to buy her supplies?
   A the library
   B the school
   C the book store
   D her room

4. What does Isabel *not* need to organize?
   F her desk
   G her room
   H her backpack
   J her closet

5. What does Isabel plan to buy with some of her money?
   A tennis shoes
   B a magazine
   C some clothes
   D some paper

Spanish 1 ¡Ven conmigo!, Chapter 2 — Standardized Assessment Tutor 5

Nombre _____ Clase _____ Fecha _____

B. Today was the first day of classes at Colegio San Vicente, and Raúl needs to go shopping for his school supplies. Read the conversation between Raúl and his mom. Answer the following questions based on the dialogue. (20 points)

MAMÁ   ¡Buenas tardes, mi hijo! ¿Cómo estás?
RAÚL   Bien. Buenas tardes, mamá.
MAMÁ   Raúl, ¿tienes una lista de las cosas que necesitas para la escuela?
RAÚL   Sí, tengo la lista con las cosas que necesito comprar.
MAMÁ   ¿Qué hay en la lista?
RAÚL   Hay bolígrafos, tres carpetas, un diccionario para la clase de inglés, una regla y unos lápices.
MAMÁ   Hay muchas cosas en la lista. Primero, vamos al centro comercial y a la librería.
RAÚL   Bueno. Mamá, quiero comprar una mochila también pero no tengo mucho dinero.
MAMÁ   No sé. ¿Cuántos dólares tienes?
RAÚL   Ya tengo cinco dólares y necesito cinco más.
MAMÁ   Bueno, Raúl.
RAÚL   Gracias, mamá.

6 What does Raúl have when he arrives home from school?
  A a new backpack
  B three folders
  C a list of school supplies that he needs to buy
  D a dictionary for English class

7 What does Raúl *not* have to get for school?
  F a calculator
  G some folders
  H pencils
  J a ruler

8 Where are Raúl and his mom going to buy the supplies?
  A the mall
  B a department store
  C school
  D the library

9 What does Raúl want to buy for himself?
  F some new jeans
  G a backpack
  H a calculator
  J a French dictionary

10 How much money does Raúl have?
  A $10
  B $15
  C $5
  D none

Nombre _____ Clase _____ Fecha _____

C. Lupe has to write a report describing her room. Read her report and answer the questions that follow. (20 points)

> Tengo el cuarto muy organizado. Tengo muchas cosas. Hay ropa en el armario. Tengo un reloj y muchas revistas en mi escritorio. Hay un radio y quiero comprar un televisor. Hay dos lámparas y muchos carteles.
>
> Me gusta mucho mi cuarto pero necesito hacer la cama.

11 What type of person is Lupe?
A   rich
B   unorganized
C   organized
D   a good student

12 Where are Lupe's clothes?
F   on the desk
G   under the bed
H   in the closet
J   lying around the room

13 What does Lupe have on her desk?
A   two lamps
B   a lot of posters
C   a television
D   a lot of magazines

14 What does Lupe want to buy?
F   a clock
G   a radio
H   a television
J   some magazines

15 What does Lupe need to do?
A   put her clothes in the closet
B   make her bed
C   her homework
D   organize her room

CAPÍTULO 2

Nombre _____ Clase _____ Fecha _____

II. Writing   (Maximum score: 40 points)

Answer the following questions in the space provided.

16 Persuasive writing It is the first day of school, and you arrive home with a list of materials that you need to buy at the book store. The list must include at least five things that you will buy. Tell your mom that you need money to buy these things. Tell her where you will buy these items. Also inform her that you want to be more organized this school year. You should write at least five sentences. (15 points)

_____
_____
_____
_____
_____

17 Descriptive writing You have just moved to a new house. Write a phone conversation with your best friend in your old school describing what you need to do in your new room. Don't forget to begin the conversation by asking how he or she is doing! Tell your friend that you are not organized in your new room, and then tell your friend about three items that you need to organize. Tell your friend that you need to clean your room right now. (15 points)

TÚ _____

TU AMIGO(A) _____

TÚ _____

TU AMIGO(A) _____

TÚ _____

TU AMIGO(A) _____

TÚ Y TU AMIGO(A) ¡Chao!

18 Narrative writing Write a letter to your grandmother telling her that tomorrow is the first day of school and you don't have a backpack for school. Tell her that you are very unorganized; that there are pens and papers in the closet, a ruler on the desk, and several books on the bed. Your calculator is on the television. Be sure to ask her how she is doing. (10 points)

Querida abuelita,

_____
_____
_____
_____

Con cariño,

Nombre _____ Clase _____ Fecha _____

Nuevas clases, nuevos amigos

I. Reading
(Maximum score: 60 points)

A. Read Alicia's letter to her friend María Inés and answer the questions that follow. (20 points)

> Querida María Inés,
>   Hola, ¿cómo estás? ¿Cómo son tus clases? Yo tengo algunas clases que me gustan mucho. Por la mañana tengo matemáticas, francés y geografía. Luego por la tarde tengo ciencias sociales, arte y educación física. El arte y el francés son mis clases favoritas. ¿Cuál es tu clase favorita?
>   Me gusta también la clase de geografía porque el profesor es interesante. Es cómico y la clase es divertida. ¿Cómo son tus profesores?
>   Bueno, tengo la clase de ciencias sociales a las cuatro y media y estoy atrasada. Un abrazo.
>
>   Tu amiga,
>   Alicia

1 Which class does Alicia have in the morning?
- A French
- B art
- C gym
- D social studies

2 Which classes does Alicia have in the afternoon?
- F math and French
- G social studies and art
- H geography
- J science

3 What is one of Alicia's favorite classes?
- A geography
- B art
- C physical education
- D math

4 Why does Alicia like her geography class?
- F The material is interesting.
- G The teacher is interesting and amusing.
- H The teacher arrives late.
- J The teacher is young.

5 Why is Alicia in a hurry?
- A She wants to talk to her teacher.
- B She is late to art class.
- C She is late to social studies class.
- D She needs to see her friend before class.

Spanish 1 ¡Ven conmigo!, Chapter 3   Standardized Assessment Tutor **9**

Nombre _____ Clase _____ Fecha _____

B. Read María Inés's response to a letter from her friend Alicia. Then, choose the answer that best completes each of the statements that follow. (20 points)

> Querida Alicia,
> ¡Hola! ¿Cómo estás? Estoy bien. Así que tienes clases interesantes, ¿eh? ¡Qué bien!
> Yo también tengo clases que me gustan. Mi materia favorita es el inglés. La profesora es estricta pero muy inteligente. También me gusta la clase de computación porque el profesor es simpático. No me gusta mucho la clase de francés, pues el profesor es aburrido y los exámenes son difíciles.
> Bueno, ya son las diez y necesito ir a la clase de matemáticas. Hasta pronto.
>
> Un abrazo,
> María Inés

6 Which subject does María Inés like best?
- A computer science
- B French
- C English
- D math

7 Why doesn't María Inés like her French class?
- F The tests are hard.
- G It's too early in the morning.
- H There is too much homework.
- J The teacher is strict.

8 Which teacher is boring?
- A math
- B English
- C computer science
- D French

9 Which class does María Inés have in the morning?
- F English
- G math
- H French
- J computer science

10 What is the teacher in María Inés's favorite class like?
- A boring
- B gives hard tests
- C nice
- D strict but very intelligent

10 Standardized Assessment Tutor

Spanish 1 ¡Ven conmigo!, Chapter 3

Nombre _____ Clase _____ Fecha _____

C. Read this description of Gaby's schedule. Then, choose the letter of the best answer to each of the questions that follow. (20 points)

> Hoy Gaby tiene siete clases. Primero tiene la clase de geografía. Luego, también por la mañana, tiene francés y ciencias sociales. El almuerzo es a las doce y media. Después, por la tarde tiene ciencias, educación física, matemáticas y por fin, arte.

11 How many classes does Gaby have today?
   A six
   B seven
   C four
   D eight

12 Which class does Gaby have first?
   F math
   G art
   H geography
   J French

13 When does Gaby have lunch?
   A at 12:30
   B before French class
   C after math class
   D before social studies

14 Which class does Gaby *not* have in the morning?
   F social studies
   G geography
   H French
   J science

15 What is Gaby's last class of the day?
   A geography
   B social studies
   C math
   D art

Nombre _____ Clase _____ Fecha _____

II. Writing
(Maximum score: 40 points)

Answer the following questions in the space provided.

16 Expository (compare and contrast) Write a description of your favorite class and your least favorite class. Tell why you like or dislike each class. Describe the teacher in each class and say one good and one bad trait for each teacher. (20 points)

_____
_____
_____
_____
_____
_____
_____

17 Persuasive There is a contest for the best student in your Spanish class. Write five sentences describing the traits that would persuade the students to vote for you. (10 points)

_____
_____
_____
_____
_____
_____
_____

18 Descriptive Describe your school schedule for this year. Include your morning classes in order, what time you have lunch, and your afternoon classes in order. (10 points)

_____
_____
_____
_____
_____
_____
_____

Nombre _____ Clase _____ Fecha _____

CAPÍTULO 4 ¿Qué haces esta tarde?

I. Reading (Maximum score: 60 points)

A. Read Carlota's responses to a class survey. Then, answer the sentences that follow. (20 points)

1 **A mí me gusta más...**
   ___ escuchar música
   ___ dar un paseo
   _X_ ir al cine
   ___ hablar por teléfono

2 **Después de clases me gusta...**
   ___ dibujar
   _X_ descansar
   ___ tomar un refresco
   ___ hablar con mis amigos

3 **Antes de mis clases tengo que...**
   ___ sacar la basura
   ___ lavar la ropa
   ___ cuidar a mi hermano
   _X_ caminar con el perro

4 **Nunca quiero...**
   ___ ir al centro comercial
   _X_ lavar el carro
   ___ hablar por teléfono
   ___ hacer la tarea

5 **El fin de semana quiero...**
   ___ estudiar
   ___ escuchar música
   ___ ir al centro comercial
   _X_ pasar el rato con amigos

1 What is Carlota's favorite activity?
  A drawing
  B washing the clothes
  C doing homework
  D going to the movies

2 What does Carlota like to do after school?
  F talk on the phone with her friends
  G go to the mall
  H rest
  J listen to music

3 What does Carlota have to do before school?
  A do her homework
  B take out the trash
  C take care of her little brother
  D walk the dog

4 What is Carlota's least favorite activity?
  F washing the car
  G listening to music
  H walking the dog
  J doing homework

5 What does Carlota like to do on weekends?
  A study
  B watch television
  C spend time with her friends
  D shop

Spanish 1 ¡Ven conmigo!, Chapter 4

Nombre _____ Clase _____ Fecha _____

B. Read the two pen pal ads below and answer the questions that follow. (20 points)

> **Nombre:** Juan Dos Santos
> **Edad:** 15 años
> **Dirección:** 55 mts. sur Bomba Gasotica, Pérez Zeledón, COSTA RICA.
> **Pasatiempos:** Escuchar música rock, hablar con amigos y tener amigos.

> **Nombre:** Wilmer Ramírez
> **Edad:** 16 años
> **Dirección:** Urb. Las Batallas, Calle La Puerta #2, San Félix, Edo. Bolívar, VENEZUELA
> **Pasatiempos:** Escuchar música, escribir cartas y estudiar.

6. Which leisure activity do Juan Dos Santos and Wilmer Ramírez have in common?
   A listening to music
   B studying
   C writing letters
   D being with their friends

7. Which is *not* a true statement about Juan Dos Santos?
   F He is younger than Wilmer.
   G He is from South America.
   H He lives in Pérez Zeledón.
   J He is very sociable.

8. Which is *not* a true statement about Wilmer Ramírez?
   A He likes to listen to music.
   B He is from South America.
   C He lives in the suburbs of Costa Rica.
   D He is older than Juan.

9. Which statement might Juan make that tells you he is more sociable than Wilmer?
   F "Tengo quince años."
   G "Me gusta escuchar música."
   H "Vivo en Costa Rica."
   J "Me gusta hablar con amigos y tener amigos."

10. Which statement might Wilmer make that tells you he is probably a good student?
    A "Tengo dieciséis años."
    B "Me gusta estudiar."
    C "Me gusta escuchar música."
    D "Vivo en Las Batallas."

C. Ana has just returned home from school. Read the note her mother left her and answer the questions that follow. (20 points)

> Ana,
> Necesito ir de compras al centro. Voy a regresar a las cinco a preparar la cena. Hay mucho que hacer antes de ir a la clase de baile a las seis. Necesitas lavar la ropa que está al lado del armario en tu cuarto. También necesitas sacar la basura que está debajo del escritorio y tienes que practicar el piano por veinte minutos. Gracias, hija.
>
> Hasta pronto,
> Mamá

11 Where is Ana's mom going?
  A to a piano lesson
  B to a dance class
  C to wash the clothes
  D shopping

12 What time will Ana's mom return home?
  F in 20 minutes
  G at 6 o'clock
  H at 5 o'clock
  J after her piano lesson

13 Which of the following does Ana *not* have to do?
  A prepare supper
  B practice the piano
  C take out the trash
  D wash the clothes

14 Where is the trash?
  F in the kitchen
  G next to the closet
  H under the desk
  J near the piano

15 When does Ana have dance class?
  A in 20 minutes
  B at 5 o'clock
  C at 6 o'clock
  D after she goes shopping with her mom

Nombre _____ Clase _____ Fecha _____

II. Writing

(Maximum score: 40 points)

Answer the following questions in the space provided.

16 Descriptive You are tired of the arrangement of your bedroom. Write a letter to your aunt, an interior decorator, explaining that you plan to organize your room. Tell her that you want to put the bed near the window, the desk next to the bed, the lamp on top of the television, and the chair beside the door. Ask her if she likes the arrangement. (20 points)

Querida tía,

_____
_____
_____
_____
_____

Tu sobrino(a),

17 Narrative You need more free time, so you write out a plan for time management. Write down each day of the week except for the weekend. Next to each day write down what you have to do before or after school. Be sure to include two jobs, besides homework, that you have to do to help around the house, including the time you plan to do the chore. (10 points)

_____
_____
_____
_____
_____
_____

18 Persuasive You are going on a day trip with some friends. Leave a note to your older brother convincing him to come with you. Write five fun activities that you have planned for the day. Also tell him what time you are leaving and returning. (10 points)

_____
_____
_____
_____
_____
_____

CAPÍTULO 5 — El ritmo de la vida

I. Reading   (Maximum score: 60 points)

A. Armando has just moved to Colorado from California. Read the letter he has written to his friend Ignacio back in California. Then, answer the questions that follow. (20 points)

> 5 de enero, 2001
> Denver, Colorado
>
> Querido Ignacio,
>   Pues, compañero, ¿qué tal? ¿Cómo estás? ¿Todavía nadas en el océano con tus amigos Carmen y Pablo? ¿Con qué frecuencia nadan en el océano? Hace frío aquí todos los días y nieva mucho.
>   Me gusta el colegio. Tengo unos nuevos amigos y jugamos al baloncesto tres veces a la semana. También esquío todos los fines de semana con un grupo del colegio. Me gusta también correr en el parque, pero hoy nadie quiere correr conmigo — está a treinta grados y está nevando. Por eso estoy en casa escribiendo cartas.
>   Bueno, hombre, hasta pronto.
>
>   Tu amigo,
>   Armando

1. Which is *not* a description of the weather in Denver?
   A snowing
   B 30 degrees
   C cold
   D warm

2. What does Armando like to do on the weekends?
   F ski
   G play basketball
   H swim in the ocean
   J study

3. What does Armando do in the park?
   A run
   B write letters
   C play basketball
   D ski

4. Who are Carmen and Pablo?
   F Armando's new friends
   G students in the new school in Colorado
   H Ignacio's friends
   J Ignacio's sister and brother

5. Why is Armando staying at home and witing letters?
   A He misses his friends.
   B He doesn't have time during the week.
   C No one wants to run with him because of the weather.
   D He writes to his friends every day.

Nombre _____ Clase _____ Fecha _____

B. Read Ignacio's reply to Armando's letter. Then, choose the correct answer to the following questions. (20 points)

> 1 de febrero, 2001
> Monterey, CA
>
> Querido Armando,
>   Entonces, amigo, ¿está nevando allá todavía? Hace muy mal tiempo allá, ¿verdad? Y yo, muy lejos de la nieve, estoy al lado de la piscina. Muchas veces Carmen, Pablo y yo nadamos en el océano. Hace muy buen tiempo—tengo muchas clases, pero a veces buceo o juego al tenis, especialmente los fines de semana. La playa es fantástica—no hay días nublados nunca.
>   Quiero oír más de tu nuevo deporte de esquiar. ¿Con qué frecuencia esquías? Escribe otra vez sobre tu colegio y tus nuevos amigos.
>   Hasta luego,
>   Ignacio

6 What is the weather like in California?
  A snowing
  B awful
  C nice
  D cloudy

7 Where do Ignacio and his friends *not* spend their time?
  F at the ocean
  G at the park
  H at the beach
  J by the swimming pool

8 What does Ignacio do on the weekend?
  A play tennis
  B ski
  C swim
  D run

9 Where is Ignacio writing the letter to Armando?
  F on the weekend
  G at the beach
  H at school
  J at the pool

10 What is Ignacio interested in hearing more about?
  A the weather
  B the beach
  C Armando's friend Pablo
  D Armando's new sport, skiing

Nombre _____ Clase _____ Fecha _____

C. Read the following phone conversation between Roberto and Carlota. Answer the following questions about their conversation. (20 points)

ROBERTO   Buenas noches, Carlota. ¿Cómo estás esta noche?
CARLOTA   Bien, gracias. ¿Y tú? ¿Qué haces?
ROBERTO   Ahora, descanso. Es el fin de semana y voy a asistir a la fiesta de María. ¿Quieres ir conmigo?
CARLOTA   Sí. Vamos juntos. ¿Cuándo es?
ROBERTO   Es mañana sábado por la noche.
CARLOTA   ¿A qué hora?
ROBERTO   Es a las nueve.
CARLOTA   ¿Dónde vive ella?
ROBERTO   Ella vive cerca del Parque Benito Juárez.
CARLOTA   Bueno, sí. Me gustaría ir contigo.
ROBERTO   ¡Fantástico! Voy a estar en tu casa a las ocho de la noche. Como es febrero, casi siempre hace frío por la noche. Necesitamos tomar un autobús.
CARLOTA   Está bien. Adiós.
ROBERTO   Hasta mañana.

11 What is Robert doing now?
  A resting
  B reading
  C his homework
  D going to María's party

12 When is María's party?
  F Friday night
  G Sunday morning
  H Saturday morning
  J Saturday night

13 Where does María live?
  A near the bus stop
  B near the park
  C far from the park
  D near Carlota's house

14 What time will Roberto come to take Carlota to the party?
  F at 9 p.m.
  G at 8 p.m.
  H this weekend
  J Saturday night

15 What will the weather probably be like?
  A hot
  B cool
  C rainy
  D cold

Nombre _____ Clase _____ Fecha _____

II. Writing (Maximum score: 40 points)

Answer the following questions in the space provided.

16 Expository (cause and effect) Write a description of five different activiites that you would do when it is hot, when it is cold, when it snows, when it is windy, and when it rains. (15 points)

_____
_____
_____
_____
_____
_____

17 Persuasive Write a letter to a friend telling him or her that not much is happening. Ask if he or she wants to spend a week with you during June or July during summer vacation. Include three activities that you both can do during the visit. Don't forget to include a date on the letter. (15 points)

_____

_____,

_____
_____
_____
_____
_____

Tu amigo/a

18 Descriptive Write a sentence for each season of the year, including the months of that season and an activity that you like to do in the morning and during the afternoon during that season. (10 points)

_____
_____
_____
_____
_____
_____

CAPÍTULO 5

CAPÍTULO 6
Entre familia

I. Reading

(Maximum score: 60 points)

A. Florencia wants a summer job as a camp counselor. When she applied at Camp Nuevas Fronteras, they asked her to write a paragraph about herself and her family. Read the paragraph she wrote below. Then, choose the letter of the best answer to each of the questions that follow. (20 points)

> Me llamo Florencia Rodríguez y soy del Ecuador. Tengo quince años y me gusta jugar al tenis y trabajar en el jardín. Me gusta también tocar la guitarra, pero debo practicar más. Vivo en un apartamento en el centro de Quito con mi familia. Somos seis—mi mamá, mi papá, mis hermanos Daniel y Pilar y nuestra abuela. Daniel tiene veinte años y Pilar tiene dieciocho. Yo soy la menor de los hermanos. Tenemos un gato en casa también. Se llama Nieve porque es blanco como la nieve.

1 How old is Florencia?
  A 18
  B 15
  C 20
  D 6

2 Who is the oldest in Florencia's family?
  F Nieve
  G Florencia
  H Pilar
  J Daniel

3 What does Florencia need to do more often?
  A play with her cat
  B play tennis
  C practice the guitar
  D work in the garden

4 What color is Florencia's cat?
  F white
  G black
  H grey
  J yellow

5 Which is *not* a true statement about Florencia's family?
  A They live in the center of Quito.
  B They live in an apartment.
  C Her grandmother lives with them.
  D There are four children in the family.

Nombre _____ Clase _____ Fecha _____

B. When Eugenio woke up on Saturday morning, he found this note from his older sister, María. After you read the note, choose the letter of the best answer to each of the questions below. (20 points)

> ¡Buenos días, hermanito Eugenio!
> Mañana los tíos comen en casa con nosotros; por eso ustedes necesitan hacer muchas cosas hoy. Leticia necesita lavar y planchar la ropa. Néstor necesita limpiar la cocina y pasar la aspiradora por toda la casa. Tú debes sacar la basura y cortar el césped. Salgo del trabajo a las cuatro y quiero ver la casa bien limpia.
> María

6. Who is coming to visit?
   A   Leticia
   B   their aunt and uncle
   C   María
   D   Néstor

7. Who has to wash and iron the clothing?
   F   Néstor
   G   María
   H   Leticia
   J   Eugenio

8. When will the company arrive?
   A   at 4 o'clock
   B   tomorrow
   C   this morning
   D   tomorrow morning

9. Who has to mow the lawn?
   F   María
   G   Néstor
   H   Leticia
   J   Eugenio

10. When will María be home?
    A   tomorrow morning
    B   soon
    C   at 4 o'clock
    D   at noon

Nombre _____ Clase _____ Fecha _____

C. Mrs. González is very stressed and writes a letter for advice to Dear Abby. Read the lettter and then answer the following questions about her problems. (20 points)

> Querida Abby,
>
> Tengo un problema. Mi esposo y yo tenemos una familia muy grande. Somos seis y yo tengo demasiado trabajo. Mis quehaceres domésticos son limpiar la casa, lavar y planchar la ropa, preparar la comida, trabajar en el jardín y cuidar los gatos. Mi esposo va a su trabajo todos los días, pasa la aspiradora y corta el césped.
>
> El problema es que tenemos cuatro gatos. Clarita es muy traviesa y Paquito es un poco gordo. Él come mucho. Clarita es menor que Paquito. Ellos son muy cariñosos. Lolita es muy vieja y a ella no le gusta salir de la casa. Anita, la menor de todos, tiene los ojos verdes. Ella es blanca y también es mi favorita.
>
> ¡Ayúdame! ¿Qué debo hacer?
>
> Sra. María Elena González

11 How many persons live in the González household?
A four
B two
C six
D eight

12 What chore does Mrs. González *not* have to do?
F prepare the meals
G mow the lawn
H the laundry
J care for the pets

13 Which cat is mischievous?
A Anita
B Paquito
C Lolita
D Clarita

14 Which cat is the youngest?
F Anita
G Paquito
H Lolita
J Clarita

15 Which cat is very old?
A Anita
B Paquito
C Lolita
D Clarita

Nombre _____ Clase _____ Fecha _____

II. Writing

(Maximum score: 40 points)

Answer the following questions in the space provided.

16 Narrative Ana's mother left a note explaining what Ana, her younger sister, and her older brother need to do when they arrive home from school. Write the note that her mother left, including two household chores that each one needs to do before her mother arrives at 5:30 PM. (20 points)

Ana,

_____
_____
_____
_____
_____
_____

       Gracias,
       Mami

17 Descriptive Describe your family, including name, age, a physical description, and a character description of each one. Be sure to include yourself. Start by saying how many are in your family. (10 points)

_____
_____
_____
_____
_____
_____

18 Persuasive Write a letter to your grandmother. Tell her that you have a problem. Mom says that she has too much work. List five household chores that Mom does. Tell her that Mom needs a rest but explain that you do help with the chores. Tell your grandmother that you want to see all your family soon. (10 points)

Querida abuelita,

_____
_____
_____
_____

Gracias, abuelita. Hasta pronto.
     Tu nieto/a,

Nombre _____ Clase _____ Fecha _____

Math (Maximum score: 100 points)

The temperatures on the chart below are given in degrees Celsius. Use the formula $T_F = \frac{9}{5} t_c + 32.0$ to convert temperatures from Celsius to Fahrenheit. (T_F = temperature in Fahrenheit; t_c = temperature in Celsius) Round to the nearest degree.

PRONÓSTICO: ESPAÑA   el 18 de marzo

Ciudad	hoy mínimo/máximo °C	mañana mínimo/máximo °C
La Coruña	15/19	15/17
Barcelona	14/20	13/25
Córdoba	9/24	9/25
Jaén	6/22	7/24
Madrid	12/17	11/19
Málaga	10/23	11/26
Sevilla	11/24	10/25
Valencia	17/21	17/23

1 What is the high temperature for tomorrow in Sevilla?
 A 43° F
 B 52° F
 C 75° F
 D 77° F

2 What is the low temperature for tomorrow in Madrid?
 F 52° F
 G 57° F
 H 63° F
 J 84° F

3 What is the low temperature for tomorrow in La Coruña?
 A 47° F
 B 59° F
 C 63° F
 D 40° F

4 What is the high temperature for Córdoba today?
 F 75° F
 G 77° F
 H 39° F
 J 58° F

Nombre _____ Clase _____ Fecha _____

5 What is the high temperature for Barcelona for tomorrow?
  A 77° F
  B 68° F
  C 45° F
  D 36° F

6 What is the low temperature for Valencia for today?
  F 73° F
  G 70° F
  H 63° F
  J 49° F

7 What is the high temperature for Málaga for today?
  A 79° F
  B 52° F
  C 73° F
  D 55° F

8 What is the low temperature for Málaga for today?
  F 43° F
  G 37° F
  H 50° F
  J 52° F

9 What is the low temperature for Jaén for tomorrow?
  A 43° F
  B 39° F
  C 45° F
  D 72° F

10 What is the high temperature for Madrid for tomorrow?
  F 66° F
  G 63° F
  H 52° F
  J 54° F

CAPÍTULO 7 ¿Qué te gustaría hacer?

I. Reading
(Maximum score: 60 points)

A. Read the note below. Then answer the questions that follow. (20 points)

> Querida Yolanda,
> ¡Felicidades! ¡Qué bien que te gradúes este año! Yo también tengo muchas ganas de graduarme.
> Es una lástima, pero no puedo ir a tu fiesta. El veinticinco de mayo tengo que ir a la fiesta de cumpleaños de mi primo Quique, el que vive en Concepción, pero sé que ustedes lo van a pasar muy bien. Paso por tu casa mañana para llevar un regalo.
> Amanda Narváez Gijón

1. Why is Amanda congratulating Yolanda?
   - A It is Yolanda's birthday.
   - B Yolanda is having a birthday party.
   - C Yolanda is graduating.
   - D Yolanda is moving to Concepción.

2. Why is Amanda going to visit Yolanda tomorrow?
   - F She is bringing her a gift.
   - G She is coming to her birthday party.
   - H She is coming to her graduation party.
   - J She needs to pick up her cousin Quique.

3. When is Yolanda graduating?
   - A tomorrow
   - B this year
   - C on May 25th
   - D next year

4. Who is celebrating a birthday?
   - F Concepción
   - G Yolanda
   - H Amanda
   - J Quique

5. Why is Amanda unable to attend Yolanda's party?
   - A She has to attend Concepción's graduation.
   - B She has to attend her cousin's graduation.
   - C She has to go to her cousin's birthday party.
   - D She can't afford a gift for Yolanda.

Nombre _____ Clase _____ Fecha _____

B. Read this telephone conversation. Then answer the questions that follow. (20 points)

LALO   Aló.
PABLO   Hola Lalo, soy Pablo.
LALO   Hombre, Pablo, ¿qué tal?
PABLO   Bien, ¿y tú?
LALO   Muy bien. ¿Qué pasa?
PABLO   Oye, vamos el sábado a mi casa de campo. ¿Quieres ir?
LALO   ¿Cuándo? ¿El sábado? Pues, sí, me gustaría ir. ¿A qué hora piensan salir?
PABLO   A las once. Queremos pescar y jugar al fútbol. A ti te gusta jugar al fútbol, ¿verdad?
LALO   Que sí, hombre.
PABLO   Pues, lo vamos a pasar muy bien. Bueno, ¿te llamo el sábado, entonces?
LALO   Sí, a las diez. ¿Está bien?
PABLO   Perfecto. Hasta el sábado. Chao, Lalo.

6 Where does Pablo invite Lalo to go?
    A to play football
    B to a party
    C to go camping
    D to his home in the country

7 When are they going?
    F Saturday
    G Wednesday
    H Friday
    J Sunday

8 What do they *not* plan to do?
    A fish
    B camp
    C play soccer
    D have a good time

9 What time are they leaving?
    F 10 a.m.
    G 11 p.m.
    H 11 a.m.
    J Pablo will call later with the time.

10 Which statement is true for Lalo?
    A He has a house in the country.
    B He calls up his friend.
    C He likes to play soccer.
    D He doesn't like to fish.

C. Graciela wants to get a group of friends together to go to the movies, but she isn't having much luck. Read what she says. Then, answer the questions that follow. (20 points)

> Quiero ir al cine a ver *El monte de terror* el sábado por la noche. No me gustaría ir sola, pero todo el mundo ya tiene planes. Manolo no puede ir porque va al circo con sus padres. Lupita va a pasar el fin de semana en el campo y Matilde tiene que trabajar. Luisa no está en casa, y a Chusa, su hermana, no le gustan las películas de terror *(scary movies)*. Tonio y Sonia van al Vegas Burger a cenar y no quieren ir al cine. Bueno, llamo otra vez a casa de Luisa a ver si está.

11 What does Graciela want to do Saturday night?
- **A** go to the circus
- **B** go to a movie
- **C** go to a restaurant
- **D** her homework

12 Who is going to the country?
- **F** Matilde
- **G** Tonio y Sonia
- **H** Lupita
- **J** Manolo

13 Who has to work?
- **A** Manolo
- **B** Chusa
- **C** Luisa
- **D** Matilde

14 Who doesn't like scary movies?
- **F** Chusa
- **G** Graciela
- **H** Manolo
- **J** Matilde

15 Who isn't home right now?
- **A** Lupita
- **B** Luisa
- **C** Manolo
- **D** Tonio and Sonia

Nombre _____ Clase _____ Fecha _____

II. Writing (Maximum score: 40 points)

Answer the following questions in the space provided.

16 Persuasive Write a letter to a friend inviting him or her to visit you. Include a date for the visit. Talk about three activities that you plan to do during the visit. Mention that you will have a wonderful time. Say that if there is time and money you can do another activity. Tell your friend to answer soon. (20 points)

_____
_____
_____
_____
_____
_____

17 Descriptive Write a description of your daily personal hygiene routine. Include five activities, stating which one you do first and continue from there. (10 points)

_____
_____
_____
_____
_____
_____

18 Narrative Write a telephone conversation. Begin with the appropriate greetings, and then ask who is calling. Say to whom you would like to speak. Say that the other person isn't there. Ask if you can leave a message and then say farewell. (10 points)

_____
_____
_____
_____
_____
_____

CAPÍTULO 8

¡A comer!

I. Reading (Maximum score: 60 points)

A. Some room-service bills have gotten mixed up at the hotel where Ángel is working. Read over the four bills below, and then help Ángel decide which bill goes to which customer. (20 points)

```
Marta Susana Martínez
pescado                        7.000
huevos revueltos con queso     5.500
café                             500
                              13.000
```

```
Ramiro Álvarez
pollo asado                    6.500
legumbres                      1.000
huevos revueltos con queso     5.500
agua mineral                     750
                              13.750
```

```
Alejandro Sánchez
ensalada de pollo              5.000
frijoles                       1.000
2 cafés                        1.000
                               7.000
```

```
Olga Santos
carne colorada                 5.500
legumbres                      1.000
huevos revueltos con queso     5.500
limonada                         500
                              12.000
```

1 Which customer ordered a dish made with beef?
  A Marta Martínez
  B Alejandro Sánchez
  C Ramiro Álvarez
  D Olga Santos

2 Which customer ordered fish?
  F Marta Martínez
  G Alejandro Sánchez
  H Ramiro Álvarez
  J Olga Santos

3 Which customer ordered the roast chicken?
  A Marta Martínez
  B Alejandro Sánchez
  C Ramiro Álvarez
  D Olga Santos

4 Which customer did *not* order the scrambled eggs with cheese?
  F Marta Martínez
  G Alejandro Sánchez
  H Ramiro Álvarez
  J Olga Santos

5 Who had the most expensive meal?
  A Marta
  B Alejandro
  C Ramiro
  D Olga

Spanish 1 ¡Ven conmigo!, Chapter 8

Nombre _____ Clase _____ Fecha _____

B. Read the following conversation. Then answer the following questions based on the conversation. (20 points)

CAMARERO	Buenas tardes. Bienvenidos a nuestro restaurante. Aquí tienen el menú.
MARI LUZ	Muchas gracias.
BENI	Muchas gracias.
	(más tarde)
CAMARERO	¿Qué les puedo traer?
MARI LUZ	Tengo mucha hambre. Quisiera pedir una hamburguesa con queso, lechuga y papitas. Pero no quiero cebollas. No me gustan. Y para tomar, un vaso de leche.
CAMARERO	¿Y Ud. señor?
BENI	Quisiera algo más ligero. Voy a pedir una ensalada de camarones, y un plato de frutas tropicales, pero no con papaya. No me gusta. Y voy a tomar una limonada con la comida.
CAMARERO	¿Algo más?
BENI	Ahora, no.
	(una hora más tarde)
BENI	Señor, la cuenta por favor. ¿Está incluida la propina?
CAMARERO	No, es aparte.
BENI	Gracias.

6 What does Mari Luz *not* want with her hamburger?
- A onion
- B cheese
- C lettuce
- D potato chips

7 What beverage does Mari Luz order?
- F a cup of coffee
- G a glass of milk
- H juice
- J no beverage

8 What is Beni *not* ordering for lunch?
- A shrimp salad
- B fruit salad
- C milk
- D lemonade

9 What type of fruit does Beni *not* like?
- F pineapple
- G oranges
- H bananas
- J papaya

10 What is *not* included in the bill?
- A the drinks
- B the tip
- C the fruit salad
- D the potato chips

Nombre _____ Clase _____ Fecha _____

C. Katrina and Gobi have planned to have dinner together. Read the conversation, and then answer the questions that follow. (20 points)

KATRINA ¿Cómo es el West Indian Café? ¿Preparan comidas ricas?
GOBI Sí, preparan comidas riquísimas. Su especialidad son platos típicos del Caribe.
KATRINA ¿Qué comen en el Caribe?
GOBI Pues, comen mucho pescado, camarones, frutas tropicales, batidos de frutas, plátanos fritos...
KATRINA ¡Plátanos fritos! ¡Qué horrible!
GOBI Pues, son muy ricos, Katrina, te van a gustar.
KATRINA No sé. ¿Por qué no vamos a otro restaurante? Podemos ir al Pollo Flaco, pues no me gusta para nada el pescado, pero el pollo sí me gusta mucho.
GOBI Tienen pollo en el West Indian Café. También tienen ensaladas, frijoles, carne, cabrito *(goat)*...
KATRINA ¡Ay, cabrito no, por favor! No me gustan los frijoles tampoco. Las ensaladas y las frutas me encantan, pero la carne no me gusta mucho.
GOBI Mira los platos del día, a ver si tienen algo que te guste.

11 Where does Katrina want to eat?
  A at the Pollo Flaco
  B in the Caribbean
  C at the West Indian Café
  D none of the above

12 What is the speciality of the West Indian Café?
  F fish
  G goat
  H Caribbean food
  J chicken

13 Which is *not* a food served at the West Indian Café?
  A smoothies
  B fish
  C fried bananas
  D special rice dishes

14 What suggestion does Gobi offer?
  F that they go to another restaurant
  G that they try the goat and fried bananas
  H that they order the chicken
  J that they look at the menu

15 What is one of Katrina's favorite foods?
  A chicken
  B fried bananas
  C fish
  D goat

Nombre _____ Clase _____ Fecha _____

II. Writing   (Maximum score: 40 points)

Answer the following questions in the space provided.

16 Expository (compare and contrast) Write a comparison of two restaurants. Tell what kind of food each offers including the specialty. Tell when you like to go there (special occasion). Mention whether the food is expensive or not and what you generally order at each restaurant. (20 points)

_____
_____
_____
_____
_____
_____
_____

17 Descriptive Describe how to set a table for a family meal. Include the main dishes (plate, bowl, glass) with the usual utensils and where each would be placed. (10 points)

_____
_____
_____
_____
_____
_____
_____

18 Persuasive Write a note to a friend and persuade him or her to go to lunch with you to your favorite restaurant because it is your birthday. Tell him or her what type of food they serve, including their specialty. Tell what you always order and that they have wonderful desserts. (10 points)

_____
_____
_____
_____
_____
_____
_____

Nombre _____ Clase _____ Fecha _____

CAPÍTULO 9

¡Vamos de compras!

I. Reading
(Maximum score: 60 points)

A. Read this letter that you have received from a friend in Guadalajara, Mexico. Then, answer the questions that follow. (20 points)

> Querido Joe,
>
> ¡Hola! Quiero escribirte porque hoy es la fiesta de cumpleaños de mi hermana, Rosa. Todos los amigos de Rosa van a venir para ayudar a celebrar este día importante. Creo que le van a regalar a Rosa muchas cosas bonitas. Por ejemplo, Martín tiene ganas de darle una radio nueva, y Leonor quiere invitar a Rosa a almorzar en su restaurante favorito.
>
> Ahora, yo tengo que pensar en un regalo bonito para Rosa, pues es mi hermana. A mí me gustan los discos compactos y los juegos de mesa, y a Rosa también le encantan. Bueno, Joe, tengo prisa. Escríbeme, por favor.
>
> Un abrazo,
> Lorenzo

1 Who is celebrating a birthday?
  A Joe
  B Lorenzo
  C Martín
  D Rosa

2 Who wants to give the birthday person a new radio?
  F Lorenzo
  G Martín
  H Rosa
  J Leonor

3 What is Rosa's brother's name?
  A Joe
  B Martín
  C Lorenzo
  D Leonor

4 Where does Leonor want to invite Rosa to go?
  F shopping
  G to a birthday party
  H to her favorite restaurant
  J to a movie

5 What will Lorenzo probably give Rosa as a gift?
  A CDs and a board game
  B a new radio
  C lunch at a nice restaurant
  D new clothes

Spanish 1 ¡Ven conmigo!, Chapter 9   Standardized Assessment Tutor

Nombre _____ Clase _____ Fecha _____

B. Read the following brochure about shopping possibilities in San Antonio. Answer the questions that follow. (20 points)

> **SAN ANTONIO:** ¿Listo para ir de compras? Usted puede tomar un taxi acuático al divertido centro comercial al lado del Paseo del Río. Es posible encontrar verdaderos tesoros *(treasures)* en los centros comerciales de la ciudad. En la Villita y El Mercado, usted puede ver todo tipo de artesanías. Usted puede encontrar todo lo que le gusta—tenemos una gran variedad de almacenes, joyerías, jugueterías y pastelerías. En el distrito comercial de San Antonio, usted va a pasarlo bien. Y después, puede comer en uno de los muchos restaurantes del área. Usted y su familia pueden comer parrilladas al estilo tejano y platos mexicanos muy picosos. Hay también comida oriental, continental y "alta cocina americana". ¡Hay de todo para la diversión de usted y su familia!

6 According to the article, how can you get to the mall area of San Antonio?
  A by water taxi
  B by trolley
  C by car
  D by bus

7 What are "la Villita" and "El Mercado"?
  F hotels
  G restaurants
  H shopping malls
  J airports

8 Which is something *not* mentioned that you can buy in San Antonio?
  A toys
  B jewelry
  C records
  D pastries

9 Which is a type of restaurant *not* mentioned in the article?
  F Mexican
  G Italian
  H Chinese
  J American

10 Which dish is mentioned in the article?
  A San Antonio-style hamburgers
  B Texas-style barbeque
  C fried rice
  D pizza

Nombre _____ Clase _____ Fecha _____

C. Lorenzo and his friend Daniel are shopping for a birthday present for Rosa, Lorenzo's sister. Read their conversation, then answer the questions that follow. (20 points)

LORENZO ¿Cuál de esas blusas prefieres, Daniel, la blusa roja o la de cuadros?
DANIEL Yo prefiero la roja. ¿Cuánto cuesta?
LORENZO Uy, cien dólares. Es cara.
DANIEL ¿Qué te parecen estos pantalones cortos?
LORENZO Eh... de verdad, Daniel, no me gustan las rayas. Parecen ser de los años setenta.
DANIEL ¿Qué tal esta falda? Sólo cuesta doce dólares. Es una ganga.
LORENZO No sé. Prefiero regalarle algo divertido. ¿Por qué no vamos a buscar algo diferente?
DANIEL Muy bien. Vamos a buscar una tarjeta.

11 What do Lorenzo and Daniel buy?
  A a blouse
  B a skirt
  C nothing yet
  D some shorts

12 Which blouse does Daniel prefer?
  F the plaid one
  G the striped one
  H the red one
  J none of them

13 How much does the blouse cost?
  A 70 dollars
  B 7 dollars
  C 100 dollars
  D 12 dollars

14 What does Lorenzo want to buy?
  F a blouse
  G a skirt
  H a pair of shorts
  J something fun

15 What do the two of them decide to look for?
  A a different red blouse
  B something less expensive
  C a card
  D a skirt

Nombre _____ Clase _____ Fecha _____

II. Writing   (Maximum score: 40 points)

Answer the following questions in the space provided.

16 Expository (compare and contrast) Write a comparison of what you wear when the weather is cold and when the weather is hot. Write at least five sentences (10 points)

_____
_____
_____
_____
_____
_____
_____

17 Descriptive You are shopping for your family on Christmas *(la Navidad)*. Describe what you would give your grandparents, your parents, an older brother, and a younger sister. Include one descriptive word for each item that you buy and where you would buy two of the presents. (15 points)

_____
_____
_____
_____
_____
_____
_____

18 Narrative Your family just won a trip to the Caribbean Islands. Write a letter to a friend telling him or her what you will pack in your suitcase. Say that you want to take comfortable clothes. Imagine that you will visit museums, different restaurants, disco clubs, and, of course, the beach. (10 points)

_____
_____
_____
_____
_____
_____
_____
_____

Celebraciones

I. Reading
(Maximum score: 60 points)

A. Read the following passage, and then answer the following questions. (20 points)

El día de Ernesto empieza a las ocho de la mañana. Le gusta afeitarse y ducharse temprano, pero no tiene prisa, porque hoy es sábado. Habla con su amigo Reynaldo por teléfono y después mira un partido de fútbol en la televisión. Luego lee el periódico y juega con el perro, Plutón.

Mira el reloj. Son las once. ¡Ay, no!—piensa Ernesto—Hoy tengo el examen especial de matemáticas, y ¡empieza ahora mismo!

Ernesto va al teléfono para llamar a la universidad. Si no toma el examen hoy, no puede asistir al curso de verano de la universidad.

1 When does Ernesto's day begin?
- A at 8:30 A.M.
- B at 8:00 A.M.
- C at 7:30 A.M.
- D at 11:00 A.M.

2 Which is *not* one of Ernesto's morning activities?
- F watching a soccer game
- G shaving
- H showering
- J playing soccer

3 What did Ernesto forget to do?
- A to call his professor
- B to go take his math test
- C to walk his dog
- D to attend his summer school class

4 What time is Ernesto's math test?
- F 11 A.M.
- G 10 A.M.
- H 8 A.M.
- J 3 P.M.

5 What plans does Ernesto have for the summer?
- A play soccer with his friend Reynaldo
- B take his math test
- C attend summer school
- D read the newspaper and play with his dog

Nombre _____ Clase _____ Fecha _____

B. Read the following letter that Susana wrote to Norma. Then answer the questions that follow. (20 points)

> Querida Norma,
>   ¿Qué tal pasaste la Navidad? Mis padres y yo pasamos la Navidad con mi tía Julia en San Antonio. Es una ciudad muy bonita. Visitamos el Álamo, el famoso Paseo del Río y el zoológico. Almorzamos y cenamos en unos restaurantes muy buenos. A mí me encanta la comida de aquí; se llama comida Tex-Mex. A papá no le gusta, pues a él no le gusta la comida picante, pero a mí me gusta mucho.
>   También visitamos un centro comercial fabuloso y mamá compró un suéter muy bonito para mi tía. ¡Qué sorpresa al abrir los regalos en la celebración de la Nochebuena! El suéter que mamá le compró a mi tía Julia era igual que el suéter que mi tía Julia le compró a mamá. Compraron el mismo suéter en la misma tienda.
>   Sé que estás muy ocupada, pero me gustaría saber qué tal pasaste las vacaciones. Escribe pronto.
>   Tu amiga,
>   Susana

6 Which is *not* a place that Susana and her parents visit in San Antonio?
 A the Alamo
 B Tex-Mex
 C the Riverwalk
 D the zoo

7 What does Susana's dad *not* like?
 F San Antonio
 G her aunt
 H spicy food
 J Christmas

8 What did Susana's mom buy at the mall?
 A shoes for her husband
 B Tex-Mex food
 C a sweater for Julia
 D tickets to the zoo

9 What is the coincidence with Susana's mom and her aunt?
 F They like the same type of food.
 G They both dislike Tex-Mex food.
 H They both open their gifts on Christmas morning.
 J They bought each other the same gift at the same store.

10 Which statement is true?
 A Susana's aunt Julia is visiting them for Christmas.
 B Susana's father does *not* like the restaurants on the Riverwalk.
 C Susana's friend Norma is very busy during the holidays.
 D Susana's mother doesn't like the spicy food in San Antonio.

C. Read this paragraph. Then answer the questions that follow. (20 points)

Juan celebró el día de su santo con una fiesta en casa de sus abuelos. Invitó a todos sus compañeros de clase. Isa e Hilda decoraron el patio con globos azules y rojos y compraron una piñata para los niños. Tomás sacó fotos de todo el mundo. Doña Clementina, la abuela de Juan, preparó los platos que más le gustan a Juan. Mirta tocó el piano y yo canté.

11 Where does Juan plan to celebrate his saint's day?
- A at his home
- B at his friend's home
- C at his grandparent's home
- D at a restaurant

12 Who decorated the patio?
- F Mirta
- G Isa and Hilda
- H his grandmother
- J Tomás

13 Who took pictures?
- A Clementina
- B Juan
- C Mirta
- D Tomás

14 Who prepared the food?
- F Juan and his mom
- G Tomás
- H Juan's grandmother
- J Isa and Hilda

15 Who played the piano at Juan's party?
- A his grandparents
- B Mirta
- C Juan
- D Isa and Hilda

Nombre _____ Clase _____ Fecha _____

II. Writing

(Maximum score: 40 points)

Answer the following questions in the space provided.

16 Descriptive Linda calls her friend Anita to plan a New Year's Eve party. Anita's mom answers the phone, so Linda has to ask for Anita, who then comes to the phone. Write the conversation in which Linda discusses what she is planning to do to get ready for the party. Include several things that Linda is planning to do. At the end, Linda asks Anita to come to her house and help her. (15 points)

_____
_____
_____
_____
_____
_____

17 Persuasive Tomorrow is Soledad's birthday and her mom has a lot to do to get ready. She leaves a note for Soledad's dad. Write the note that Soledad's mom leaves. (10 points)
Include
- an apology saying that at this moment she is very busy
- five commands (familiar) of things that she wants him to do to get ready for the party
- a thank you for the help

_____
_____
_____
_____
_____
_____

18 Narrative Write a description of what happened at Soledad's birthday party. (15 points)
Include
- when you attended
- that you had a good time
- what you gave her
- three things that you did at the party

_____
_____
_____
_____
_____
_____

CAPÍTULO 10

Nombre _____ Clase _____ Fecha _____

CAPÍTULO 11 Para vivir bien

I. Reading
(Maximum score: 60 points)

A. Read this conversation carefully. Then, choose the best answer to each question. (20 points)

JULIA ¿Qué te pasa, Elena? ¿Te puedo ayudar?
ELENA Sí. Ayúdame con la mochila, por favor. Me duelen los brazos. Anteayer fui al gimnasio y levanté pesas por demasiado tiempo. Ahora no puedo jugar bien al voleibol.

1 How does Elena want Julia to help her?
   A by lifting her feet
   B by getting her weights that she left in the gym
   C by playing volleyball for her
   D by carrying her backpack for her

2 Where is Elena sore?
   F her back
   G her feet
   H her arms
   J her hand

3 Why is Elena so sore?
   A She fell yesterday.
   B She played too much volleyball.
   C She carried too much weight in her backpack yesterday.
   D She overdid it lifting weights.

4 When did Elena go to the gym?
   F today
   G yesterday
   H last night
   J the day before yesterday

5 What is Elena worried about *not* being able to do now?
   A lift weights
   B go to the gym
   C play volleyball well
   D go to school

Spanish 1 ¡Ven conmigo!, Chapter 11   Standardized Assessment Tutor **43**

Nombre _____ Clase _____ Fecha _____

B. Read this conversation carefully. Then, choose the best answer to each question. (20 points)

GABRIELA Lo pasé muy bien el fin de semana pasado. Fui a ver el partido de béisbol. Ganó mi colegio.

ARTURO Catalina y yo fuimos al cine a ver "El Rey León". Nos gustó bastante. Y tú, Beatriz, ¿qué hiciste?

BEATRIZ Mi familia y yo fuimos al campo el domingo e hicimos un picnic. Comimos bocadillos de atún. Más tarde preparamos pollo a la parrilla. Y luego, celebramos el cumpleaños de mi primo con un pastel.

6 What baseball game did Gabriela go to?
 A her friend's
 B her nephew's
 C her boyfriend's
 D her school's

7 What happened to Gabriela's baseball team?
 F They lost.
 G There was a tie.
 H They won.
 J The game was cancelled.

8 What did Arturo do this weekend?
 A He stayed at home
 B He went to the zoo.
 C He went to the museum.
 D He went to the movies.

9 Where did Beatriz go with her family?
 F to the country
 G to the park
 H camping
 J to their lake house

10 What did Beatriz's family *not* eat at the picnic?
 A barbequed chicken
 B cake
 C tuna sandwiches
 D pasta

Nombre _____ Clase _____ Fecha _____

C. Read the following conversation between Benjamín and his mom. Answer the questions that follow. (20 points)

BENJAMÍN Ay, mamá.
MAMÁ ¿Qué tienes, hijo? ¿Te sientes mal?
BENJAMÍN Sí, me siento muy mal. Debo tener gripe.
MAMÁ ¿Y, por qué dices eso?
BENJAMÍN Porque tengo fiebre y tos.
MAMÁ ¿Y la garganta?
BENJAMÍN Me duele mucho. Me duele todo el cuerpo.
MAMÁ Estoy preocupada pero probablemente estás resfriado y nada más. Pero, ¿qué tal si te llevo al médico esta tarde?

11 What does Benjamín think is wrong with him?
 A He has the flu.
 B He has a cold.
 C He has something really bad.
 D He is only tired.

12 What hurts Benjamín?
 F his entire body
 G his head
 H his nose
 J his back

13 What symptom does Benjamín *not* have?
 A a cough
 B a fever
 C body aches
 D a tooth ache

14 What does Benjamín's mom think the problem probably is?
 F He has the flu.
 G He has a cold.
 H He has a headache.
 J He is just tired.

15 Where does Benjamín's mom suggest they go this afternoon?
 A to the movies
 B to his dad's office
 C to the zoo
 D to the doctor

CAPÍTULO 11

Spanish 1 ¡Ven conmigo!, Chapter 11

Nombre _____ Clase _____ Fecha _____

II. Writing
(Maximum score: 40 points)

Answer the following questions in the space provided.

16 Descriptive Write a description of what you did during the week. Include five things that you did, when you did them, and where you did them. (20 points)

_____
_____
_____
_____
_____
_____

17 Narrative You don't feel well and think that you might have the flu. Leave your mom a note telling her (10 points)
- you don't feel well and are in your bedroom resting
- you think that you have the flu
- three symptoms that you have
- you want to go to the doctor today

_____
_____
_____
_____
_____
_____

18 Persuasive Write a report persuading someone to change his or her lifestyle and get in better shape. (10 points)
Include
- what exercise to do and how often
- eating habits
- rest

Say that you will help him or her do these things.

_____
_____
_____
_____
_____
_____
_____

Nombre _____ Clase _____ Fecha _____

CAPÍTULO 12

Las vacaciones ideales

I. Reading
(Maximum score: 60 points)

A. Alfonso wrote out his daily schedule. Read the schedule, then use it to answer the questions that follow. (20 points)

> Horario semanal de Alfonso Berea Valcarce
>
> De lunes a viernes me despierto a las siete y media.
> Desayuno — me gusta tomar un jugo de naranja y cereal con leche — y voy a clases. Primero tengo la clase de matemáticas. La segunda clase es la de geografía.
> Entonces tengo un descanso de quince minutos.
> Después del descanso tengo una clase más antes del almuerzo: la historia del arte. Luego, tengo cuatro clases más: historia, lengua española, inglés y biología. Mi clase favorita es la biología.

1. What time does Alfonso wake up?
   A at 8 A.M.
   B at 7 A.M.
   C at 7:30 A.M.
   D at 6:30 A.M.

2. What does Alfonso like to eat for breakfast?
   F toast with jelly and a cup of coffee
   G orange juice and cereal with milk
   H He doesn't usually have time for breakfast.
   J eggs with bacon and hot chocolate

3. Where does Alfonso go after he eats breakfast?
   A to class
   B to his friend's house
   C to the university
   D to soccer practice

4. Which class does Alfonso have first?
   F art history
   G English
   H math
   J biology

5. How long is Alfonso's break between classes?
   A He doesn't take a break.
   B five minutes
   C fifteen minutes
   D thirty minutes

Spanish 1 ¡Ven conmigo!, Chapter 12   Standardized Assessment Tutor 47

Nombre _____ Clase _____ Fecha _____

B. Read the vacation itinerary for TurUSA below. Based on the itinerary, answer the questions that follow. (20 points)

TurUSA—Viajes organizados a EE.UU.

Día 1: Llegada a Washington, D.C. a las 8:00 de la mañana. Viaje en autobús al Hotel Presidente Washington. Recorrido en autobús por la hermosa ciudad de Washington, D.C. Excursión a las tiendas de Washington Square por la tarde. Cena a las 19.00 h.

Día 2: Desayuno continental en el hotel. Viaje en metro al Cementerio Nacional de Arlington. Recorrido con guía por el cementerio y también visita a la Casa del General Lee y a la Tumba del Soldado Desconocido. Almuerzo en el restaurante Riverside. Tarde libre. Excursión de noche al barrio encantador de "Old Town Alexandria".

---

6 Where are the tourists *not* going on the first day?
 A Washington Square
 B the Tomb of the Unknown Soldier
 C a tour of the city
 D the Hotel President Washington

7 How are the tourists going to see the sights of the city on Day 1?
 F by bus
 G by taxi
 H by metro
 J by car

8 When do the tourists have time to do whatever they want to do?
 A on the first morning
 B on the second morning
 C on the first afternoon
 D on the second afternoon

9 Where are the tourists going the second night?
 F to General Lee's Home
 G to the Tomb of the Unknown Soldier
 H Old Town Alexandria
 J National Cemetery

10 When do the tourists eat at The Riverside restaurant?
 A at 8 a.m. on the first day
 B at 7 p.m. on the first day
 C noon on the second day
 D on the second night

Nombre _____ Clase _____ Fecha _____

C. Read the following letter that Mónica wrote to her brother about her recent vacation. Answer the questions that follow. (20 points)

> Querido hermano,
> ¿Qué tal? Estoy de muy buen humor y te escribo para decirte de mis vacaciones fantásticas. Fui a Francia por quince días. Lo pasé muy bien. Visité París donde hay muchos museos. Los restaurantes allí son increíbles. También pasé dos días en la playa donde nadé, tomé el sol y salté en paracaídas. Fue muy divertido. Por las mañanas fui de vela en el Mar Mediterráneo. Fue un paraíso.
> Visité las montañas por tres días con unos amigos. Hace mucho frío en los Pirineos. Esquié y escalé las montañas.
> Ahora estoy en casa y estoy muy cansada pero necesitas venir a verme. Saqué unas fotos maravillosas. Nos vemos pronto.
>
> Tu hermana,
> Mónica

11 How long was Mónica's vacation?
 A a week
 B two weeks
 C a month
 D a year

12 Where did Mónica go on her vacation?
 F Italy
 G Germany
 H France
 J England

13 How long did Mónica spend at the beach?
 A 12 days
 B 15 days
 C 2 days
 D a week

14 What did Mónica do in the mountains?
 F She went skydiving.
 G She sunbathed.
 H She visited lots of museums.
 J She went skiing and climbing.

15 Why does Mónica want her brother to visit her?
 A to see her new house
 B to talk about climbing
 C to show him photos of her trip
 D to discuss their upcoming vacation

Spanish 1 ¡Ven conmigo!, Chapter 12 Standardized Assessment Tutor

Nombre _____ Clase _____ Fecha _____

II. Writing

(Maximum score: 40 points)

Answer the following questions in the space provided.

16 Narrative Write a letter to a friend saying that you are very sad because you don't get to take a vacation during spring break. Say what you feel like doing but you can't because you have to stay home, and it is so boring. (15 points)

_____
_____
_____
_____
_____
_____

17 Expository (compare and contrast) Your family wants to take a summer vacation but they can't decide whether to go to the beach or to the mountains. Write a report for your Spanish class describing the benefits of each place. Include four things that you can do at each place, how the weather will be different in each place, and the difference in the clothing that you will have to take to each place. (15 points)

_____
_____
_____
_____
_____
_____
_____

18 Descriptive Write a description of a perfect vacation spot. (10 points)
Include
- where you are going and why you chose this type of trip
- what you plan to pack for the trip
- what you plan to do on the trip
- how long you will be gone and when you will return

_____
_____
_____
_____
_____
_____
_____
_____

Nombre _____ Clase _____ Fecha _____

Math Test 2   (Maximum score: 100 points)

Use the conversion chart below to answer questions based on the graph that follows the chart. Round your answers to the nearest whole number.

HEIGHT	WEIGHT
1 meter = 39.37 inches	1 kilo = 2.2 pounds
100 centimers = 1 meter	1000 grams = 1 kilo

The following graph uses the metric system to show some Spanish students' height and weight.

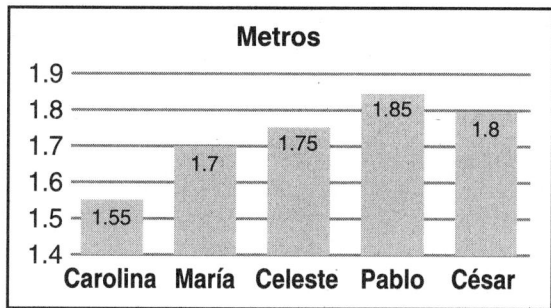
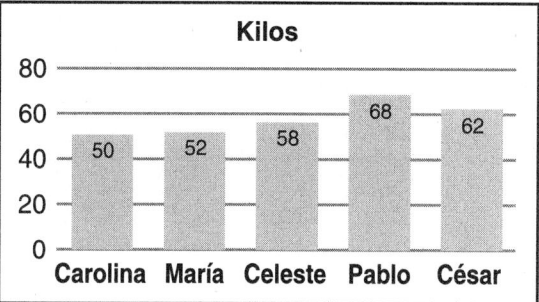

1 How tall is Carolina?
 A 4'11"
 B 5'1"
 C 5'2"
 D 5'3"

2 How much does Carolina weigh?
 F 105 lbs.
 G 110 lbs.
 H 112 lbs.
 J 114 lbs.

3 How tall is César?
 A 5'9"
 B 5'11"
 C 6'1"
 D 6'2"

4 How much does César weigh?
 F 136 lbs.
 G 140 lbs.
 H 143 lbs.
 J 145 lbs.

Spanish 1 ¡Ven conmigo!   Standardized Assessment Tutor

5 How tall is María?
- A 5'4"
- B 5'5"
- C 5'7"
- D 5'8"

6 How much does María weigh?
- F 114 lbs.
- G 117 lbs.
- H 121 lbs.
- J 125 lbs.

7 How tall is Pablo?
- A 5'10"
- B 5'11"
- C 6'1"
- D 6'4"

8 How much does Pablo weigh?
- F 150 lbs.
- G 154 lbs.
- H 156 lbs.
- J 160 lbs.

9 How tall is Celeste?
- A 5'8"
- B 5'9"
- C 5'10"
- D 5'11"

10 How much does Celeste weigh?
- F 120 lbs.
- G 128 lbs.
- H 131 lbs.
- J 135 lbs.

Score Sheet and Answers

Nombre _____ Clase _____ Fecha _____

Spanish 1 ¡Ven conmigo!
Standardized Assessment Tutor

Reading

1 Ⓐ Ⓑ Ⓒ Ⓓ   6 Ⓐ Ⓑ Ⓒ Ⓓ   11 Ⓐ Ⓑ Ⓒ Ⓓ
2 Ⓕ Ⓖ Ⓗ Ⓙ   7 Ⓕ Ⓖ Ⓗ Ⓙ   12 Ⓕ Ⓖ Ⓗ Ⓙ
3 Ⓐ Ⓑ Ⓒ Ⓓ   8 Ⓐ Ⓑ Ⓒ Ⓓ   13 Ⓐ Ⓑ Ⓒ Ⓓ
4 Ⓕ Ⓖ Ⓗ Ⓙ   9 Ⓕ Ⓖ Ⓗ Ⓙ   14 Ⓕ Ⓖ Ⓗ Ⓙ
5 Ⓐ Ⓑ Ⓒ Ⓓ   10 Ⓐ Ⓑ Ⓒ Ⓓ   15 Ⓐ Ⓑ Ⓒ Ⓓ

Writing

16 _____

_____

_____

_____

_____

_____

_____

_____

_____

_____

17 _____

_____

_____

_____

_____

_____

_____

_____

_____

_____

18 _____

_____

_____

_____

_____

_____

_____

_____

_____

Math

1 Ⓐ Ⓑ Ⓒ Ⓓ   5 Ⓐ Ⓑ Ⓒ Ⓓ   9 Ⓐ Ⓑ Ⓒ Ⓓ
2 Ⓕ Ⓖ Ⓗ Ⓙ   6 Ⓕ Ⓖ Ⓗ Ⓙ   10 Ⓕ Ⓖ Ⓗ Ⓙ
3 Ⓐ Ⓑ Ⓒ Ⓓ   7 Ⓐ Ⓑ Ⓒ Ⓓ
4 Ⓕ Ⓖ Ⓗ Ⓙ   8 Ⓕ Ⓖ Ⓗ Ⓙ

Answers

CAPÍTULO 1

1 C
2 F
3 C
4 J
5 D
6 B
7 G
8 C
9 J
10 B
11 B
12 J
13 B
14 B
15 A

16 Answers will vary. Example:
Me llamo … (Soy …; Mi nombre es …)
Tengo … años.
Soy de …
Me gusta mucho el/la (deporte) pero no me gusta (mucho) el/la (deporte).
Me gusta el/la (comida) pero no me gusta mucho el/la (comida).

17 Answers will vary. Example:
Querido(a) ,
¡Hola! ¿Cómo estás? Me llamo … Tengo … años. Soy de …
Me gusta (mucho/más) el/la … pero no me gusta el/la …
¿Y tú? ¿Cuántos años tienes? ¿Qué te gusta?
                    Adiós.

18 Answers will vary. Example:
Me llamo … (Mi nombre es …/ Yo soy …)
Tengo … años.
Yo soy de …
Me gusta el/la … y el/la … pero no me gusta ni el/la … ni el/la …

CAPÍTULO 2

1 D
2 H
3 C
4 H
5 B
6 C
7 F
8 A
9 G
10 C
11 C
12 H
13 D
14 H
15 B

16 Answers will vary. Example:
TÚ   Mamá, aquí tengo la lista de cosas que necesito comprar.
Necesito comprar un(a) …, un(a) … y un(a) … También un(a) … y un(a) … Necesito el dinero para ir a la librería para comprar las cosas. Quiero ser más organizado(a). Gracias, mamá.

17 Answers will vary. Example:
TÚ   ¡Hola! ¿Qué tal?
AMIGO(A)   Bien. ¿Y tu nuevo cuarto?
TÚ   Fantástico. Necesito hacer muchas cosas. Necesito poner la ropa en el armario, hacer la cama y poner la nueva lámpara en el escritorio. Mi cuarto es un desastre.
AMIGO(A)   Mañana es el primer día de clases, ¿no?
TÚ   Sí, necesito irme. Chao.
AMIGO(A)   Sí, chao.

18 Answers will vary. Example:
Querida abuelita,
¿Cómo estás? Mañana es el primer día de clases. Necesito una mochila, pero no tengo dinero. Necesito organizar mis cosas. Hay lápices y papeles en el armario, hay una regla en el escritorio y unos libros en mi cama. También hay una calculadora en la télévision.

Spanish 1 ¡Ven conmigo!   Standardized Assessment Tutor

CAPÍTULO 3

1. A
2. G
3. B
4. G
5. C
6. C
7. F
8. D
9. G
10. D
11. B
12. H
13. A
14. J
15. D
16. Answers will vary. Example:
    Mi clase favorita es ... pero no me gusta la clase de ...
    Me gusta la clase de ... porque es muy fácil pero no me gusta la clase de ... porque los exámenes son difíciles.
    Mi profesora de la clase de ... es muy interesante pero muy estricta.
    Mi profesor de la clase de ... es aburrido y da mucha tarea.
17. Answers will vary. Example:
    Me llamo ... y yo quiero ser tu estudiante favorito(a). ¿Por qué?
    Soy un(a) buen(a) estudiante.
    Soy divertido(a) y simpático(a)
    Soy cómico(a).
    Soy inteligente e interesante.
18. Answers will vary. Example:
    Mi horario
    Por la mañana primero tengo la clase de ..., luego la clase de ... y después la clase de ...
    A las ... tengo el almuerzo. Por la tarde tengo la clase de ..., entonces la clase de ... y por fin la clase de ...

CAPÍTULO 4

1. D
2. H
3. D
4. F
5. C
6. A
7. G
8. C
9. J
10. B
11. D
12. H
13. A
14. H
15. C
16. Answers will vary. Example:
    Querida tía,
    ¿Cómo estás? Quiero organizar mi cuarto y tengo un plan. Primero, voy a poner la cama cerca de la ventana. Voy a poner el escritorio al lado de la cama y la lámpara encima del televisor. Por fin voy a poner la silla al lado de la puerta. ¿Te gusta?
    Tu sobrino(a)
17. Answers will vary. Example:
    El lunes a las ... necesito sacar la basura y preparar la cena.
    El martes a las ... necesito caminar con el perro y estudiar.
    El miércoles a las ... necesito cuidar a mi hermana y practicar el piano.
    El jueves a las ... necesito organizar mi cuarto y lavar la ropa.
    El viernes a las ... necesito preparar el almuerzo y estudiar.
18. Answers will vary. Example:
    Hermano,
    Si tienes tiempo libre el fin de semana, mis amigos y yo vamos a Cuernavaca. ¿Quieres ir con nosotros? Vamos a salir a las ocho de la mañana. Primero vamos a montar en bicicleta, entonces vamos a la piscina. Luego queremos jugar al fútbol. Más tarde vamos a un restaurante y después vamos a escuchar música en el parque. Vamos a regresar a las ocho. ¿Quieres ir con nosotros?
    Chao.

CAPÍTULO 5

1 D
2 F
3 A
4 H
5 C
6 C
7 G
8 A
9 J
10 D
11 A
12 J
13 B
14 G
15 D

16 Answers will vary. Example:
Típicamente cuando hace calor yo voy a la playa o nado en la piscina.
Cuando hace frío me gusta leer una revista y descansar.
Cuando nieva (está nevando) me gusta esquiar.
Cuando hace viento yo corro (me gusta correr).
Cuando llueve (está lloviendo) me gusta pescar con mi papá.

17 Answers will vary. Example:

12 de marzo

Querido/a amigo/a,
¿Cómo estás? ¿Qué tal? No hago mucho porque hace mal tiempo pero tengo una idea. ¿Quieres pasar una semana durante junio o julio conmigo durante las vacaciones de verano? Hace buen tiempo y todos los días yo voy a la piscina y nado con mis amigos. También me gusta pescar, leer e ir al parque. Escríbeme.
Bueno, hasta pronto.
Tu amigo/a,

18 Answers will vary. Example:
Durante la primavera cuando hace buen tiempo me gusta correr en el parque por la mañana y por la tarde me gusta trabajar en el jardín. Durante el verano cuando hace calor yo voy a la playa por la mañana con mi familia y por la tarde leo un libro. Durante el otoño cuando hace fresco o hace viento me gusta jugar al fútbol por la tarde y por la mañana yo pesco con mi familia. Durante el invierno cuando hace frío yo voy a esquiar por la mañana y por la tarde me gusta hablar por teléfono con mis amigos.

CAPÍTULO 6

1 B
2 J
3 C
4 F
5 D
6 B
7 H
8 B
9 J
10 C
11 C
12 G
13 D
14 F
15 C

16 Answers will vary. Example:
Ana,
Después de clases, ustedes necesitan hacer unos quehaceres domésticos. Ana, tú debes limpiar la cocina y planchar la ropa. Tu hermano mayor necesita pasar la aspiradora y cortar el césped. Tu hermana menor debe cuidar al gato y poner la mesa. Regreso a las cinco y media. Gracias.
Mami

17 Answers will vary. Example:
Somos cuatro en mi familia. Mi mamá se llama Ana y tiene treinta y ocho años. Mi papá se llama Raúl y tiene cuarenta años. Mi hermano tiene ocho años y se llama Francisco. Me llamo Lupe y tengo quince años. Mi mamá es delgada y muy cariñosa. Mi papá tiene los ojos negros como yo y es muy listo. Mi hermanito es un poco gordo y muy travieso. ¿Y yo? Yo soy pelirroja y muy inteligente.

18 Answers will vary. Example:
Querida abuelita,
¿Cómo estás? ¿Y abuelito? Tengo un problema. Mi mamá dice que tiene demasiado trabajo y necesita más ayuda. Yo ayudo pero ella trabaja en el jardín, limpia la casa, prepara las comidas, lava y plancha la ropa. Quiero ver a toda la familia pronto. Adiós. Hasta pronto.
Tu nieto/a,

MATH TEST 1

1 D
2 F
3 B
4 F
5 A
6 H
7 C
8 H
9 C
10 F

CAPÍTULO 7

1 C
2 F
3 B
4 J
5 C
6 D
7 F
8 B
9 H
10 C
11 B
12 H
13 D
14 F
15 B

16 Answers will vary. Example:
Querido/a amigo/a,
¿Qué tal? ¿Cómo estás? Te invito a mi casa a visitarme. ¿Quieres venir el viernes, el 8 de agosto? Vamos a pasarlo bien. Tengo planes para ir al museo de antropología, al zoológico y también al teatro. ¿Te gusta? Si hay tiempo y tenemos dinero, vamos a ir al parque de atracciones. Bueno, te llamo más tarde.
Adiós. Chao.
Tu amigo/a,

17 Answers will vary. Example:
Todos los días yo tengo que hacer muchas cosas para estar listo/a. Primero, tengo que ducharme. Después, tengo que lavarme los dientes, afeitarme, peinarme y por fin yo necesito ponerme la ropa. Como un poco y salgo para la escuela.

18 Answers will vary. Example:
Persona A Aló.
Persona B Buenos días. Me gustaría hablar con (nombre), por favor.
Persona A ¿De parte de quién?
Persona B Soy yo, (nombre).
Persona A Lo siento, pero no está.
Persona B ¿Puedo dejar un recado?
Persona A Sí. Está bien.
Persona B (nombre) necesita hablarme.
Persona A Muy bien. Adiós.
Persona B Hasta luego.

CAPÍTULO 8

1. D
2. F
3. C
4. G
5. C
6. A
7. G
8. C
9. J
10. B
11. C
12. H
13. D
14. J
15. A

16. Answers will vary. Example:
Tengo dos restaurantes favoritos. Uno se llama Antonio's y el otro se llama El Acapulco. Antonio's sirve comida italiana y El Acapulco sirve comida mexicana. La comida en Antonio's es muy cara pero en El Acapulco no cuesta mucho. La especialidad de Antonio's es el pescado y la especialidad de El Acapulco es el pollo. Los dos son fantásticos. Voy a Antonio's cuando es mi cumpleaños porque es muy caro pero voy al restaurante El Acapulco muchas veces con mi familia.

17. Answers will vary. Example:
Para poner la mesa, tengo un plato, un tazón (plato hondo), un vaso, una cuchara, un tenedor, un cuchillo y una servilleta. Pongo el plato en el medio y el tazón encima del plato. Pongo el vaso arriba del plato y a la izquierda. La servilleta está a la izquierda y pongo el tenedor encima de la servilleta. A la derecha del plato está la cuchara y al lado de la cuchara está el cuchillo.

18. Answers will vary. Example:
Amigo/a, ¿no quieres ir conmigo a mi restaurante favorito? Es mi cumpleaños y me gustaría mucho. Tienen comida mexicana y no es muy cara. Sus platos del día son chiles rellenos, pescado y pollo asado. La comida no es muy picante. Por lo general pido el pescado con frijoles y arroz. A veces, si tengo mucha hambre, pido una ensalada. Y los postres son muy ricos. Ven conmigo, ¿no?

CAPÍTULO 9

1. D
2. G
3. C
4. H
5. A
6. A
7. H
8. C
9. G
10. B
11. C
12. H
13. C
14. J
15. C

16. Answers will vary. Example:
Cuando hace frío, yo llevo pantalones con un suéter o una chaqueta. También llevo calcetines con botas o con zapatos pero cuando hace calor, prefiero llevar unos pantalones cortos con una camiseta y sandalias.

17. Answers will vary. Example:
Voy de compras para mi familia. Para la Navidad me gustaría regalarle una corbata de seda a mi abuelo y pienso regalarle un suéter de lana a mi abuela. Ella siempre tiene frío. Le regalo una cartera de cuero a mi papá y unos zapatos a mi mamá. Voy a ir a la florería para comprarle unas flores porque le gustan mucho las flores. Para mi hermano mayor voy a ir a la tienda de discos para comprarle unos discos compactos de su grupo favorito. Necesito ir a la juguetería porque voy a regalarle un juego de mesa a mi hermana menor. ¡Vamos a tener una Navidad fantástica!

18. Answers will vary. Example:
Querido/a amigo/a,
   ¡Qué tal! No vas a creer esto. Mi familia y yo vamos a viajar al Caribe este verano. ¿Qué piensas que debo llevar conmigo? Vamos a visitar unos museos y voy a llevar una blusa y una falda. Para la playa tengo un traje de baño de rayas nuevo. Cuando vamos a los restaurantes yo puedo llevar unos pantalones cortos y una camiseta. Prefiero la ropa cómoda. Quiero ir a una discoteca con mis papás y tengo un vestido bonito que voy a llevar. ¡Va a ser fantástico! Me gustaría llevarte conmigo pero no puedo. Escríbeme.
   Tu amigo/a,

CAPÍTULO 10

1 B
2 J
3 B
4 F
5 C
6 B
7 H
8 C
9 J
10 C
11 C
12 G
13 D
14 H
15 B

16 Answers will vary. Example:
LINDA   Aló. ¿Está Anita?
MAMÁ   Buenas tardes. ¿De parte de quién?
LINDA   Soy yo, Linda Valencia, señora.
MAMÁ   Momento, por favor.
ANITA   Hola, Linda. ¿Qué tal?
LINDA   Bien. ¿Qué estás haciendo la Nochevieja? Quiero invitarte a una fiesta.
ANITA   ¡Me parece maravilloso!
LINDA   Estoy haciendo las invitaciones ahora. Creo que estoy invitando a todos nuestros amigos. Necesito preparar la comida y decorar la casa con globos de muchos colores. ¿Quieres ayudarme?
ANITA   Claro que sí.
LINDA   Bueno, ven a mi casa ahora.
ANITA   Voy en seguida. Adiós.
LINDA   Chao.

17 Answers will vary. Example:
Querido,
   Lo siento pero en este momento estoy muy ocupada. ¿Me haces el favor de ayudarme con las preparaciones para la fiesta de cumpleaños de Soledad mañana? Llama a los invitados, infla todos los globos, cuelga las decoraciones, pon la mesa y prepara los sándwiches. Gracias, mi corazón.

18 Answers will vary. Example:
El sábado pasado Soledad celebró su cumpleaños. Lo pasamos bien. Le regalé un disco compacto de su grupo favorito. Todos nosotros bailamos y cantamos mucho. Sus padres decoraron la casa con globos. ¡Qué divertido!

CAPÍTULO 11

1 D
2 H
3 D
4 J
5 C
6 D
7 H
8 D
9 J
10 D
11 A
12 F
13 D
14 G
15 D

16 Answers will vary. Example:
Durante la semana yo hice muchas cosas. El lunes fui a la biblioteca y estudié. El martes fui al gimnasio y levanté pesas. El miércoles fui al estadio para ver un partido de fútbol. Ayer fui al cine con unos amigos y hoy fui a la escuela.

17 Answers will vary. Example:
Mamá,
   No me siento nada bien. Estoy descansando en mi cuarto. Creo que tengo gripe. Me duele la cabeza, tengo tos y también tengo fiebre. Me duele todo el cuerpo. ¿Podemos ir al médico hoy? Gracias.

18 Answers will vary. Example:
Cada persona tiene la responsabilidad de cuidarse. Cada persona tiene que hacer algo para llevar una vida sana. Primero, necesita comer comida sana. También debe hacer ejercicios todos los días como levantar pesas, correr o hacer yoga. Por fin es muy importante dormir ocho horas por noche. Todo esto es muy importante para llevar una vida sana. Yo puedo ayudar. Voy a ser tu entrenador personal. Vamos a hacer ejercicios todos los días, y vamos a empezar mañana.

CAPÍTULO 12

1 C
2 G
3 A
4 H
5 C
6 B
7 F
8 D
9 H
10 C
11 B
12 H
13 C
14 J
15 C

16 Answers will vary. Example:
Querido/a amigo/a,
   ¿Cómo estás? Estoy muy triste. Son las vacaciones de primavera y hace muy buen tiempo pero mi familia y yo no vamos a ningún lugar. ¡Qué aburrido! Tengo ganas de ir a las montañas para esquiar o a la playa para ir de vela y tomar el sol. No quiero quedarme en casa y hacer nada.
   Perdóname. Como puedes ver estoy muy deprimido(a). Escríbeme.
      Tu amigo/a

17 Answers will vary. Example:
Me gusta ir de vacaciones. ¡Es muy divertido! Si vamos a las montañas podemos dar unas caminatas y tomar fotos todos los días. Es muy buen ejercicio pero hace mucho frío. Y también podemos esquiar y escalar montañas. Pero si vamos a la playa no tengo que llevar mucha ropa porque hace calor. También podemos dar unas caminatas y nadar en el mar y hacer turismo. Me gustaría saltar en paracaídas pero papá no me permite. Dice que soy muy joven.
   No sé pero los dos lugares van a ser muy interesantes.

18 Answers will vary. Example:
Tengo planes para viajar a Europa. Quiero ir a Francia porque hay grandes ciudades, montañas y playas. Me gusta una variedad de cosas. Cuando hago mi maleta tengo que poner ropa para todo tipo de tiempo. Hace frío en las montañas pero hace calor en la playa. Voy a visitar museos y necesito ropa cómoda.
   Voy a tener dos semanas de vacaciones. Voy a regresar el 15 de julio.

MATH TEST 2

1 B
2 G
3 B
4 F
5 C
6 F
7 C
8 F
9 B
10 G